# The ABC's of Business:

How to Obtain, Sustain, and Maintain Business from A-Z.

**Teia A. Acker Moore**

ATLANTA  SAVANNAH  HOUSTON

The ABC's of Business: How to Obtain, Sustain, and Maintain Business from A-Z.

**ISBN: 9798858707233**

**© Copyright 2023 Teia Alicia Acker Moore**
**Ebony & Ivory Prof. Svcs., LLC. / Moore Books, LLC.**
All photos / Illustrations by Teia Alicia Acker © 2013
Front & Back Cover designed by EIPS, INC of Atlanta, Georgia.

**Edited by Tyrone Avery Acker for T. A. Acker**
**All rights reserved.**

Reproduction or translation of any part of this work is unlawful. No part of this document may be reproduced or transmitted in any form or by any means, electronic, mechanical, photocopying, recording, or otherwise, without prior written permission of Teia Alicia Acker Moore and Ebony & Ivory Professional Services, LLC. and Moore Books, LLC.

This product is designed to provide authoritative information in regard to the subject matter covered. It is sold with the understanding that the publisher is not engage in the rendering nor is responsible for, legal, or accounting services. If legal, accounting or industry specific advice is required; the services of a competent professional in those areas should be sought

"To the visionaries, the risk-takers, and the dreamers, whose unwavering dedication and relentless pursuit of excellence have illuminated the path to success in the world of business. May your endeavors continue to inspire, innovate, and elevate, leading us toward a future defined by opportunity, growth, and achievement."

T...

To the Business Owner
You've Got This... Own It.

# Table of Contents

Forward

Preface

Introduction

Acknowledgements

| | | |
|---|---|---|
| A | Accountability = Access | 1 |
| B | Booked = Blessed, not Busy | 9 |
| C | Consistency = Currency | 17 |
| D | Distractions = Disasters | 23 |
| E | Effort = Energy | 29 |
| F | Faith = Freedom | 35 |
| G | Good Strategies = Greater Gains | 41 |
| H | Humility = Hierarchy | 47 |
| I | Inquiries = Income | 53 |
| J | Joint Ventures = Jackpot | 59 |
| K | Kneeling = Knowledge | 65 |
| L | Loyalty = Longevity | 71 |
| M | Management = Matriculation | 77 |

| | | |
|---|---|---|
| N | No = No | 83 |
| O | Order = Opportunity | 89 |
| P | Purpose = Position | 95 |
| Q | Quality = Qualified | 101 |
| R | Repetition = Revenue | 107 |
| S | Sensibility = Sustainability | 113 |
| T | Teachable = Tenacious | 119 |
| U | Uniqueness = Unlimited Opportunities | 125 |
| V | Verified = Validity | 131 |
| W | Waste Not = Want Not | 137 |
| X | eXcuses = No eXecution | 143 |
| Y | Yearning = Yielding | 149 |
| Z | Xero Investment = Zero Return | 155 |

Conclusion

About The Author

# | Foreword |

*By James L. Moore*

In the ever-evolving landscape of business, success is a symphony composed of countless notes, each representing a vital aspect that contributes to the harmonious growth of enterprises. As we embark on this enlightening journey through 'The ABC's of Business: How to Obtain, Sustain, and Maintain Business from A-Z,' we find ourselves equipped with a guide that not only unveils the intricacies of commerce but also nurtures the entrepreneurial spirit within us all.

This comprehensive volume doesn't merely lay out a roadmap; it paints a vivid portrait of the multifaceted world of business, capturing the essence of what it takes to not only survive but thrive. From the initial spark of inspiration to the sustained flame of success, each chapter resonates with the principles of accuracy, brevity, and clarity – the very qualities that define effective communication in the business realm.

Whether you're a seasoned captain of industry or a fresh-faced entrepreneur, you'll discover a treasure trove of insights within these pages. As you immerse yourself in the wisdom shared by the authors, you'll find practical strategies, illuminating stories, and

# Forward

actionable advice that can serve as your North Star on the path to achieving your business goals.

As we journey from 'A' to 'Z,' from the foundational steps to the pinnacles of accomplishment, remember that success in business is a tapestry woven from experience, knowledge, and tenacity. This book not only imparts knowledge but also kindles a sense of camaraderie, reminding us that we're all part of a dynamic ecosystem where collaboration and innovation flourish.

So, let the voyage begin. May 'The ABC's of Business' be your compass, guiding you through uncharted waters and illuminating the path to success with the brilliance of its insights. As you embrace the wisdom within these pages, may you find not only the keys to unlocking business excellence but also the inspiration to propel your aspirations to new heights.

Here's to a transformative journey and to the immeasurable potential that lies within the alphabet of business. I am so proud of my beautiful wife and the knowledge she brings to the business world. I love you, "Hunny".

# | Preface |

## "If people like you, they'll listen to you, but if they trust you, they'll do business with you"
## -Zig Ziglar

"Welcome to 'The ABC's of Business: How To Obtain, Sustain, and Maintain Business from A-Z.' In the dynamic landscape of commerce, success is a journey that requires understanding, strategy, and dedication. This comprehensive guide is your compass, navigating you through the intricate world of business with clarity and purpose.

From the inception of an idea ('A') to the zenith of growth ('Z'), this book serves as your trusted companion, offering insights into every facet of business. Explore the foundational principles of entrepreneurship, discover the art of fostering lasting relationships with customers ('C'), delve into the strategies that drive innovation ('I'), and learn how to navigate challenges with resilience ('R').

Each chapter is meticulously crafted to illuminate key concepts with accuracy ('A'), brevity ('B'), and clarity ('C'), providing you with a blueprint for

## Preface

effective communication and decision-making. Whether you're a seasoned business professional or just embarking on your entrepreneurial journey, 'The ABC's of Business' equips you with the knowledge and tools to not only thrive but to excel.

Join us on this transformative expedition as we explore the A-Z of business, unveiling the secrets to obtaining, sustaining, and maintaining success. Let's embark on this enlightening voyage together, turning each page into a stepping stone towards your business aspirations.

**Are you ready to unlock the ABCs of business excellence?**

# | Introduction |

**"There are no secrets to success. It is the result of preparation, hard work, and learning from failure"
– Colin Powell**

The ABCs of business, which typically refer to "Accuracy, Brevity, and Clarity," are essential principles for effective communication in the business world. Here's why they are important:

1. Accuracy: In business, accurate information is crucial for making informed decisions. Miscommunication or inaccuracies can lead to costly mistakes or misunderstandings. Being accurate in your communication helps build trust and credibility with colleagues, clients, and stakeholders.

2. Brevity: Business professionals are often busy and inundated with information. Communicating concisely and to the point saves time for everyone involved. Clear and succinct messages are more

## Introduction

likely to be understood and remembered, increasing efficiency and effectiveness.

3. Clarity: Clear communication eliminates confusion and ensures that your intended message is understood correctly. Ambiguity can lead to misunderstandings, missed opportunities, and even conflicts. Clarity in communication helps to convey your ideas, instructions, or proposals more effectively. While those were basic models to how and why I do business, I decided to recreate an alphabet of business clichés that would further foster principles of business.

Ultimately, the ABCs of business help streamline communication, foster better relationships, and contribute to the overall success of a business by ensuring that information is shared accurately, efficiently, and effectively.

The ABC's of Business: How to Obtain, Maintain, and Sustain Business from A-Z" offers a comprehensive exploration of the intricate world of commerce, guiding you through the essential principles that underpin success. This journey unfolds by revealing that "Accountability = Access," highlighting the profound connection between

# Introduction

taking responsibility for your actions and gaining the means to achieve your aspirations.

In this book, we delve into the core principles that empower individuals and organizations to thrive. Just as accountability opens doors, each chapter

brings to light the vital ingredients necessary for success, from strategy to innovation, and from customer relations to resilience. With each turn of the page, you'll unlock a wealth of insights and practical advice, paving the way for your journey towards business excellence.

As you navigate the dynamic landscape of commerce, remember that accountability not only grants access to opportunities but also fosters trust, credibility, and growth. By embracing the wisdom within these pages, you'll uncover the true essence of the ABC's of business and embark on a transformative voyage towards achieving your goals.

Let this book be your guide, your mentor, and your source of inspiration as you navigate the challenges and triumphs of the business world. Welcome to a world of knowledge, empowerment, and the endless potential of accountability.

**My challenge to you is to begin. Will you?**

# | Acknowledgements |

"Every opportunity I've had to work with you, I've learned something new from you. You have taught me a lot of things in business. Thanks for being a great mentor. I want to let you know (via this book) how much I appreciate you, for being a superb businessman(woman) in my life"

Thank you to:

Martha Cooper Hudson
Terry L. McCoy
Charles P. Roberson, Sr.
Lionel Brown
Marilyn McDonald
Felecia Hill

# The ABC's of Business:

How to Obtain, Sustain, and Maintain Business from A-Z.

"Leaders inspire **<u>accountability</u>** through their ability to accept responsibility before they place blame."

— Courtney Lynch

| A |

ACCOUNTABILITY = ACCESS

# Accountability = Access

Accountability and access are two important concepts that can play a significant role in obtaining, maintaining, and sustaining a business. Let's break down how they relate to each other:

## 1. Accountability:

Accountability refers to the responsibility of individuals or entities to be answerable for their actions, decisions, and results. In the context of business, accountability is crucial for several reasons:

**Ethical Behavior:** Being accountable ensures that business activities are conducted ethically and within legal boundaries.

**Quality Control:** Accountability helps maintain the quality of products and services by holding responsible parties liable for their outcomes.

**Decision-Making:** Accountability encourages informed and responsible decision-making, leading to better business strategies.

## 2. Access:

Access refers to the ability to obtain or use something. In the context of business, access can encompass various aspects:

## Accountability = Access

**Market Access:** Having access to target markets allows a business to reach its customers and distribute its products/services effectively.

**Resource Access:** Access to resources like funding, technology, skilled labor, and materials is essential for business operations.

**Information Access:** Access to relevant information, data, and insights is crucial for informed decision-making and staying competitive.

### 3. Equation of Accountability Equals Access:

The equation "accountability equals access" suggests that being accountable can lead to increased access, which in turn supports the acquisition, maintenance, and sustainability of a business:

**Credibility:** Being accountable builds trust and credibility among customers, investors, and partners. This can enhance access to funding, partnerships, and customer loyalty.

**Regulatory Compliance:** Being accountable to regulations and standards helps a business avoid legal issues, thus maintaining its operations and access to the market.

## Accountability = Access

**Transparency:** Accountability through transparent operations and reporting attracts stakeholders who

value openness, potentially providing increased access to resources.

ACCOUNTABILITY and ACCESS are interconnected in the business world. By demonstrating accountability, a business can gain access to resources, markets, and opportunities that contribute to its success and longevity.

Remember: ACCOUNTABILY = ACCESS

**Access to Resources**: When a business demonstrates a high level of accountability, it often gains better access to resources such as funding, partnerships, and talent. Investors and partners are more likely to trust and support an accountable business.

**Access to Opportunities:** Accountable businesses tend to have a reputation for reliability and integrity. This reputation can open doors to new opportunities, collaborations, and markets that might be otherwise closed to less accountable competitors.

**Access to Information:** Accountable businesses are typically more transparent in their operations. This transparency can lead to better access to market

## Accountability = Access

insights, customer feedback, and industry trends, which in turn can inform better decision-making.

**Access to Talent:** Top-tier talent is often attracted to businesses known for their accountability. These businesses are seen as stable and trustworthy employers, making it easier to attract and retain skilled employees.

**Access to Trust:** In a world where trust is a valuable commodity, accountable businesses build trust with their customers and partners. This trust can translate into greater access to a loyal customer base and enduring business relationships.

In essence, accountability is like a key that unlocks various doors and opportunities in the business world. It builds trust and credibility, which, in turn, provides access to resources, opportunities, information, talent, and the trust of stakeholders – all of which are crucial for long-term success.

"**<u>Being busy</u>** does not always mean real work. The object of all work is production or accomplishment and to either of these ends there must be forethought, system, planning, intelligence, and honest purpose, as well as perspiration. Seeming to do is not doing"

— Thomas A. Edison

| B |

BEING BOOKED = BLESSED, NOT BUSY

## Being Booked = Blessed, Not Busy

The idea that being "booked" is seen as a blessing rather than just being "busy" reflects the concept of purposeful and meaningful engagement in business. Let's explore how being booked can be equated with being blessed and how it contributes to obtaining, maintaining, and sustaining a business:

### 1. Quality over Quantity:
Being booked implies that your business has a steady flow of meaningful opportunities and engagements. Instead of being overwhelmed with a high volume of tasks (being busy), being booked means you're focused on high-quality, purposeful work that aligns with your business goals.

### 2. Demand and Value:
When you're consistently booked, it indicates a demand for your products or services. Customers and clients see value in what you offer, leading to a sustainable stream of business. This demand can result from your reputation for delivering quality, which is a blessing in terms of long-term sustainability.

### 3. Time Management:
Being booked often requires effective time management and prioritization. It means you're investing your time and efforts in areas that yield the greatest returns. This can contribute to obtaining and

## Being Booked = Blessed, Not Busy

maintaining a successful business by avoiding time wasted on less productive activities.

**4. Networking and Relationships:**
Being booked can be a result of strong networking and positive relationships with clients and partners. These relationships, built on trust and reliability, contribute to obtaining new opportunities and maintaining ongoing business connections.

**5. Adaptability and Growth:**
A business that is consistently booked needs to adapt to changing demands and growth opportunities. This adaptability is essential for long-term sustainability, as it demonstrates the ability to evolve with market trends and customer needs.

**6. Recognition of Blessings:**
Viewing being booked as a blessing rather than mere busyness reflects a mindset of gratitude and appreciation for the opportunities that come your way. Recognizing these blessings can lead to positive energy and motivation, contributing to the overall success of your business.

Being "booked" in the context of business signifies purposeful engagement, demand for your offerings, effective time management, strong relationships, adaptability, and a positive perspective on blessings.

## Being Booked = Blessed, Not Busy

This approach can lead to obtaining, maintaining, and sustaining a successful and fulfilling business.

Remember BEING BOOKED = BLESSED, not BUSY

**Booked with Opportunities:** When your business is consistently booked with clients, projects, or orders, it means you have a steady stream of opportunities. Being "booked" implies that there's demand for your products or services, which is a positive sign of market interest and potential growth.

**Stability and Income:** Being consistently booked can provide a stable income stream for your business. It means you have a predictable flow of work and revenue, which can contribute to financial stability and sustainability.

**Building Reputation:** A booked schedule can also be a reflection of a strong reputation and customer trust. When clients and customers choose to work with you repeatedly, it indicates they value your offerings and trust your business, which can lead to long-term success.

**Productivity and Utilization:** Having a full schedule can encourage productivity and efficient resource utilization within your business. It ensures that your resources, including staff and equipment, are consistently engaged and not sitting idle.

## Being Booked = Blessed, Not Busy

**Learning and Growth:** Handling a busy schedule can also be seen as an opportunity for personal and professional growth. It challenges you and your team to continually improve, innovate, and find ways to meet the demands of your clients or customers.

In essence, "Booked = Blessed" suggests that a busy schedule, when managed effectively, can be a sign of prosperity and success in business. It indicates that your business is in demand, financially stable, and has the potential for growth and continued improvement. However, it's important to manage the workload to avoid burnout and ensure that the opportunities align with your business's long-term goals.

"The secret of success is **<u>constancy</u>** of purpose."

– Benjamin Disraeli

# | C |

CONSISTENCY = CURRENCY

## Consistency = Currency

The concept of "consistency equals currency" in business highlights the idea that maintaining consistent efforts and delivering reliable value can lead to financial success and sustainability. Let's explore how consistency serves as a form of currency and contributes to obtaining, maintaining, and sustaining a business:

**1. Building Trust:**
Consistency builds trust with customers, clients, and stakeholders. When you consistently deliver quality products, services, and experiences, you establish a reputation for reliability and dependability. Trust is a valuable currency in business, as it encourages repeat business and referrals.

**2. Customer Loyalty:**
Consistent positive experiences create customer loyalty. When customers know they can rely on your business to meet their needs consistently, they are more likely to remain loyal and continue supporting your products or services.

**3. Reputation and Branding:**
Consistency in branding, messaging, and values helps establish a strong brand identity. A recognizable and consistent brand resonates with customers and differentiates your business from competitors, contributing to obtaining and maintaining a customer base.

Consistency = Currency

**4. Predictable Results:**
Consistency in business processes leads to predictable results. This is crucial for planning, resource allocation, and meeting customer expectations. Predictability enhances your ability to sustain operations and achieve desired outcomes.

**5. Operational Efficiency:**
Consistency in processes and operations improves efficiency. When you have standardized procedures that consistently yield desired results, you save time and resources, which can contribute to the financial health of the business.

**6. Market Presence:**
Consistency in marketing efforts, such as regular content creation and engagement, maintains your visibility in the market. This ongoing presence helps you attract new customers and retain existing ones.

**7. Adaptability:**
Consistency doesn't mean rigidity. It implies a commitment to adapting and evolving while maintaining a core level of quality. Businesses that consistently adapt to changing market conditions and customer preferences are better positioned to sustain success.

**8. Long-Term Relationships:**

## Consistency = Currency

Consistency in communication and engagement fosters long-term relationships with clients, partners,

and stakeholders. These relationships can lead to collaborative opportunities, referrals, and shared success.

The principle of "consistency equals currency" underscores the value of reliability, trust, customer loyalty, branding, operational efficiency, and long-term relationships. By consistently delivering value and maintaining a high standard of quality, you can obtain, maintain, and sustain a thriving business.

"You can't do big things if you're **distracted** by small things."

— Anonymous

# D

DISTRACTIONS = DISASTERS

## Distractions = Disasters

The concept of "distractions equal disaster" emphasizes that allowing distractions to take precedence over important business activities can lead to negative consequences for obtaining, maintaining, and sustaining a business. Here's how distractions can potentially result in disaster:

**1. Loss of Focus:**
Distractions divert your attention away from critical tasks that are necessary for the success of your business. This loss of focus can lead to missed opportunities, delayed projects, and a lack of progress.

**2. Decreased Productivity:**
Distractions can significantly reduce your productivity. Spending time on non-essential activities or getting sidetracked by interruptions takes away valuable time from tasks that contribute directly to business growth and sustainability.

**3. Missed Deadlines:**
Consistently giving in to distractions can lead to missed deadlines. This can affect client relationships, damage your reputation for reliability, and hinder your ability to obtain and maintain business opportunities.

**4. Quality Compromise:**
Rushing through tasks due to distractions can compromise the quality of your work. Maintaining a

## Distractions = Disasters

high standard of quality is crucial for customer satisfaction and repeat business.

**5. Strained Focus on Goals:**
Distractions can steer you away from your long-term business goals. Instead of working toward sustained growth and success, you may find yourself addressing short-term and inconsequential matters.

**6. Opportunity Costs:**
Every moment spent on distractions comes at the cost of missed opportunities. These missed opportunities could have contributed to obtaining new clients, expanding your reach, or enhancing your offerings.

**7. Stress and Burnout:**
Constantly dealing with distractions can lead to increased stress and burnout. This affects your well-being and overall business performance, making it challenging to sustain success in the long run.

**8. Negative Impact on Relationships:**
Consistently being distracted can negatively impact relationships with clients, partners, and employees. Lack of attention can lead to misunderstandings, miscommunication, and strained professional connections.

**9. Loss of Innovation and Creativity:**

## Distractions = Disasters

Distractions impede your ability to think deeply and creatively about your business. Innovations and breakthroughs often come from focused reflection and problem-solving.

Allowing distractions to take over can have disastrous effects on your business. By prioritizing focus, managing distractions, and maintaining discipline, you can ensure that you're actively working toward obtaining, maintaining, and sustaining a successful business.

"Strength and growth come only through continuous **effort** and struggle"

— Napoleon Hill

| E |

EFFORT = ENERGY

# Effort = Energy

The idea that "effort equals energy" highlights the connection between putting in dedicated effort and expending energy to obtain, maintain, and sustain a business. Here's how this principle applies:

### 1. Obtaining Business:
When you put effort into researching the market, developing a business plan, and seeking opportunities, you invest your energy into creating the foundation of your business.

### 2. Starting Operations:
Launching a business requires significant energy to set up operations, create products/services, and establish initial marketing efforts.

### 3. Building Reputation:
Effort put into delivering quality products/services and providing exceptional customer service requires ongoing energy, contributing to building a positive reputation.

### 4. Customer Acquisition:
The energy you invest in networking, marketing, and engaging with potential clients helps attract new customers and expand your business reach.

### 5. Maintaining Operations:
Regular business operations demand continuous effort and energy to ensure consistent

Effort = Energy

product/service delivery, customer support, and efficient processes.

**6. Managing Challenges:**
When facing obstacles or challenges, the effort you invest in problem-solving and adapting to change requires focused energy to overcome these hurdles.

**7. Innovation and Growth:**
Introducing new products, services, or expanding your business requires creative effort and energy to stay innovative and seize growth opportunities.

**8. Sustaining Success:**
Sustaining a successful business involves ongoing effort to maintain customer satisfaction, adapt to market shifts, and remain competitive—requiring continuous energy.

**9. Leadership and Culture:**
Nurturing a positive work culture, providing leadership, and guiding your team demand emotional and mental energy, contributing to a thriving business environment.

**10. Long-Term Vision:**
Your energy invested in aligning your business activities with your long-term vision ensures that your efforts contribute to sustained growth and fulfillment.

## Effort = Energy

"Effort equals energy" signifies the connection between the active effort you put into various aspects of your business and the energy required to achieve your goals. By understanding and embracing this principle, you can effectively obtain, maintain, and sustain a thriving business.

"**Faith** is taking the first step even when you don't see the whole staircase."

— Martin Luther King

# | F |

FAITH = FREEDOM

## Faith = Freedom

The concept that "faith equals freedom" suggests that having faith in your business endeavors can lead to a sense of liberation, allowing you to obtain, maintain, and sustain a business in a more empowered and positive way. Here's how faith can contribute to business success:

### 1. Obtaining Opportunities:
Having faith in your business idea gives you the courage to pursue opportunities that align with your vision. Believing in your concept can open doors to partnerships, investments, and collaborations that help you obtain a foothold in the market.

### 2. Overcoming Challenges:
In the face of challenges and setbacks, faith provides you with the resilience to persevere and find solutions. This determination enables you to overcome obstacles and continue moving forward.

### 3. Risk-Taking and Innovation:
Faith encourages you to take calculated risks and explore innovative approaches. Believing in your ideas allows you to step outside your comfort zone, fostering a culture of creativity and growth.

### 4. Maintaining Resilience:
Maintaining faith in your business during tough times fosters resilience. This mindset helps you weather uncertainties and changes while remaining committed to your goals.

Faith = Freedom

### 5. Building Relationships:
Faith Equals Freedom: Faith enables you to build trust-based relationships with clients, partners, and stakeholders. When people see your dedication and belief in what you offer, they're more likely to engage with your business.

### 6. Customer Satisfaction:
Your faith in your products/services translates into confidence. This confidence impacts customer satisfaction, as clients are more likely to trust and be satisfied with offerings backed by your belief.

### 7. Long-Term Vision:
Having faith in your long-term vision keeps you focused on the bigger picture. It prevents you from getting lost in short-term setbacks and supports the sustainability of your business.

### 8. Adaptability:
Faith instills the belief that you can adapt and navigate changes. This adaptability is crucial for staying relevant and sustainable in a dynamic business environment.

### 9. Positive Mindset:
Faith cultivates a positive mindset that attracts opportunities, builds enthusiasm, and encourages a can-do attitude, all of which contribute to business growth.

## Faith = Freedom

"Faith equals freedom" reflects the idea that having faith in your business journey can empower you to obtain, maintain, and sustain your venture. By believing in your vision, you create a sense of liberation that fuels determination, resilience, innovation, and positive relationships—all essential elements for business success.

"Achieve success in any area of life by identifying the optimum **strategies** and repeating them until they become habits."

— Charles J. Givens

| G |

GOOD STRATEGIES = GREATER GAINS

## Good Strategies = Greater Gains

The concept that "good strategies equal greater gains" emphasizes the importance of well-thought-out strategies in driving business success. Here's how effective strategies contribute to obtaining, maintaining, and sustaining a business:

### 1. Obtaining Business:
Well-defined strategies for market entry, target audience identification, and value proposition can help you obtain initial customers and establish a foothold in the market.

### 2. Effective Resource Allocation:
Smart resource allocation, guided by strategic planning, ensures that your investments in time, money, and personnel are directed toward activities that yield the greatest returns.

### 3. Market Positioning:
Strategic positioning helps you differentiate your business from competitors and highlights your unique value. This can lead to increased customer interest and business opportunities.

### 4. Customer Acquisition and Retention:
Strategies for customer acquisition, engagement, and retention result in greater gains as you attract and retain a loyal customer base that generates ongoing revenue.

Good Strategies = Greater Gains

**5. Innovation and Adaptation:**

Strategic innovation and adaptation to changing market conditions allow you to stay ahead of trends and capitalize on emerging opportunities for business growth.

**6. Operational Efficiency:**
Strategies for streamlining operations and optimizing processes improve efficiency, reduce costs, and contribute to greater profitability.

**7. Risk Management:**
Effective risk management strategies minimize potential losses and safeguard your business's financial health, leading to greater gains over time.

**8. Long-Term Sustainability:**
Strategies focused on long-term sustainability consider factors such as scalability, diversification, and future growth opportunities, resulting in continued gains.

**9. Expanding Market Reach:**
Strategies for expanding into new markets or demographic segments can lead to increased sales and revenue streams.

**10. Brand Value and Reputation:**
Building a strong brand and reputation through strategic branding and marketing efforts can lead to

## Good Strategies = Greater Gains

greater gains by attracting more customers and commanding premium pricing.

**11. Stakeholder Relationships:**
Strategic management of relationships with investors, partners, and stakeholders can result in greater support, collaboration, and shared success.

Good strategies play a pivotal role in every phase of a business's lifecycle—whether obtaining initial traction, maintaining momentum, or sustaining long-term growth. By carefully crafting and implementing effective strategies, you can maximize gains, seize opportunities, and ensure your business's success and longevity.

Humility = Hierarchy

"**Humility** is the solid foundation of all virtues."

— Confucius

# Humility = Hierarchy

Humility = Hierarchy

HUMILITY = HIERARCHY

# Humility = Hierarchy

The relationship between humility and hierarchy in the context of obtaining, maintaining, and sustaining a business is complex. Humility can influence the dynamics within a hierarchical structure in several ways:

### 1. Obtaining Business:
In the early stages of obtaining business, humility can help business owners listen to customer needs and adapt their offerings accordingly. This approach can attract initial clients and build a positive reputation.

### 2. Building Relationships:
Humility allows business leaders to foster authentic relationships with clients, employees, and partners within the hierarchy. This fosters trust and positive collaboration, aiding in business growth.

### 3. Effective Communication:
Leaders who approach their hierarchical roles with humility tend to communicate more openly and genuinely. This fosters better understanding and helps address issues promptly, supporting business stability.

### 4. Learning and Adaptation:
Humble leaders are often open to learning from employees and external sources, which can lead to better adaptation to changing market conditions and business needs.

Humility = Hierarchy

**5. Decision-Making:**
Humble leaders are more likely to make well-informed decisions, considering input from various levels of the hierarchy. This can lead to better decisions and ultimately contribute to business sustainability.

**6. Employee Morale:**
Leaders who show humility create a positive work environment where employees feel valued and respected. This boosts morale and can lead to increased productivity and reduced turnover.

**7. Conflict Resolution:**
Humble leaders are more skilled at resolving conflicts within the hierarchy, as they are willing to listen to different viewpoints and work towards fair solutions.

**8. Long-Term Leadership:**
Humble leaders often inspire loyalty and trust from employees, making it more likely that the hierarchy will be sustained over the long term.

Humility shouldn't be equated with relinquishing authority or compromising business decisions. While humility can positively influence hierarchy, hierarchical structures also require clear direction and decision-making.

## Humility = Hierarchy

Humility, within a hierarchical structure, can contribute to obtaining, maintaining, and sustaining a business by fostering positive relationships, effective communication, learning, employee morale, and conflict resolution. However, striking the right balance between humility and authoritative decision-making is essential for business success.

"Opportunities don't just happen; you have to **<u>inquire</u>** about them."

— Chris Grosser

INQUIRY = INCOME

## Inquiry = Income

The concept that "inquiry equals income" highlights the value of actively seeking information, feedback, and understanding in business as a means to generate income and support business success. Here's how the practice of inquiry can contribute to obtaining, maintaining, and sustaining a business:

### 1. Obtaining Business:
Initiating inquiries and asking questions about potential customers' needs and preferences helps tailor your products or services to their requirements. This increases the likelihood of obtaining their business.

### 2. Customer Engagement:
Engaging with customers through inquiries demonstrates that you value their opinions and want to provide solutions that meet their needs. This can lead to increased customer loyalty and repeat business.

### 3. Market Research:
Conducting inquiries and surveys helps gather valuable market insights that can inform your business strategies. Understanding market trends and demands leads to more informed decisions, contributing to income generation.

### 4. Product/Service Enhancement:

Inquiry = Income

Seeking feedback through inquiries enables you to refine and enhance your offerings, making them

more appealing to customers and potentially commanding higher prices.

### 5. Client Satisfaction:
Regular inquiries into client satisfaction and feedback allow you to address concerns promptly, leading to happier clients who are more likely to continue doing business with you.

### 6. Innovation and Adaptation:
Inquiring about emerging trends and customer preferences helps you stay ahead of the competition by adapting your business offerings to changing market conditions.

### 7. Customization and Personalization:
Using inquiries to understand individual customer needs allows you to offer customized solutions, enhancing customer experiences and potentially commanding premium pricing.

### 8. Building Relationships:
Regular inquiries demonstrate your commitment to building strong client relationships. This can lead to word-of-mouth referrals and recommendations, resulting in increased income.

### 9. Strategic Planning:

Inquiry = Income

Inquiries help you gather data that informs your strategic planning. Making decisions based on

accurate information enhances your ability to allocate resources effectively and generate income.

**10. Long-Term Sustainability:**
Ongoing inquiries into customer feedback, market trends, and business performance contribute to long-term business sustainability by enabling you to adapt and evolve.

The practice of inquiry in business, whether through market research, customer feedback, or engagement, is essential for obtaining, maintaining, and sustaining income. By actively seeking information and understanding, you can tailor your business strategies, offerings, and interactions to better serve your customers, resulting in increased income and long-term success.

"A **joint venture** is a partnership in which little partners are pursued by bigger partners. The bigger partner can usually supply the little partner with more growth"

— Thomas G. Stemberg

# | J |

## JOINT VENTURES = JACKPOT

# Joint Ventures = Jackpot

The idea that "joint ventures equal jackpots" suggests that collaborating with other businesses through joint ventures can lead to significant opportunities and benefits, contributing to obtaining, maintaining, and sustaining business success. Here's how joint ventures can lead to favorable outcomes in various aspects of business:

**1. Obtaining Business:**
Collaborating with established partners in joint ventures can help you access their customer base and expand your reach, increasing your chances of obtaining new business.

**2. Resource Sharing:**
Joint ventures allow businesses to pool resources, including finances, expertise, and technology, to tackle larger projects or enter new markets. This shared resource pool can lead to more significant opportunities.

**3. Market Penetration:**
Partnering with businesses that have a strong presence in your target market can provide a faster and more effective way to penetrate that market, leading to increased business opportunities.

**4. Innovation and Research & Development**

## Joint Ventures = Jackpot

Joint ventures can facilitate collaborative research and development efforts, leading to innovative products or services that stand out in the market.

### 5. Risk Sharing:
Sharing risks and costs with partners in a joint venture can help mitigate potential losses, making it easier to pursue ambitious projects or ventures that might be risky alone.

### 6. Synergies and Expertise:
Partnering with businesses that bring complementary skills and expertise can lead to synergistic effects, enhancing the quality of offerings and generating more business opportunities.

### 7. Customer Acquisition:
Access to partner businesses' customer databases can provide opportunities for cross-selling, upselling, and reaching new audiences.

### 8. Market Expansion:
Joint ventures can help your business expand into new geographic regions or industries, tapping into untapped markets for business growth.

### 9. Brand Exposure:
Collaborating with well-established brands can lead to increased brand exposure and awareness,

## Joint Ventures = Jackpot

attracting more customers and business opportunities.

**10. Long-Term Partnerships:**
Successful joint ventures can lead to long-term partnerships, providing consistent opportunities for mutual growth and sustainability.

Joint ventures provide an avenue for businesses to combine their strengths, resources, and expertise to achieve greater outcomes than they could individually. By partnering strategically, businesses can obtain new opportunities, maintain a competitive edge, and sustain growth over the long term—akin to hitting "jackpots" in the world of business.

"**<u>Knowledge</u>** is not to be taken lightly. It is to be pursued relentlessly"

— Malika E. Nura

| K |

KNEELING = KNOWLEDGE

## Kneeling = Knowledge

The comparison of "being kneeling" to "knowledge" suggests that the act of humbling oneself, seeking guidance, and being open to learning can lead to obtaining, maintaining, and sustaining a successful business. Here's how the concept of being humble and seeking knowledge can contribute to various aspects of business:

**1. Obtaining Business:**
Humility and a willingness to learn from customers and clients can help you understand their needs better, leading to improved products or services that resonate with your target audience.

**2. Customer-Centric Approach:**
Being open to customer feedback and actively seeking their opinions allows you to gather valuable insights. This knowledge can help you tailor your offerings to meet customer expectations, leading to increased business.

**3. Market Research:**
Humility encourages you to acknowledge that there's always more to learn about your industry and market. Seeking knowledge through research and staying informed about trends ensures your business remains competitive.

**4. Innovation and Adaptation:**
Acknowledging that you don't have all the answers makes you more receptive to new ideas and

## Kneeling = Knowledge

innovative approaches. This mindset allows you to adapt to changes and innovate to meet evolving customer demands.

### 5. Networking and Partnerships:
Humble interactions with potential partners and industry peers foster genuine relationships. These connections can provide knowledge-sharing opportunities, collaborations, and business growth.

### 6. Effective Decision-Making:
A humble attitude acknowledges that there's always room for improvement. This mindset leads to informed decision-making, as you seek knowledge and perspectives before making important choices.

### 7. Employee Engagement:
Being open to learning from employees and valuing their contributions fosters a positive work environment. Engaged employees are more likely to contribute to business success.

### 8. Customer Loyalty:
Demonstrating humility and a commitment to ongoing learning builds trust and loyalty with customers. This trust encourages repeat business and referrals.

### 9. Long-Term Adaptability:

## Kneeling = Knowledge

A humble approach allows you to acknowledge when a business strategy needs adjustment. This

adaptability based on new knowledge is vital for long-term sustainability.

**10. Personal and Professional Growth:**
Cultivating a mindset of humility leads to continuous personal and professional growth. This growth positively influences your business decisions and strategies.

The act of "being kneeling" metaphorically represents the humility and willingness to seek knowledge, feedback, and understanding. By embracing this approach, you can obtain valuable insights, maintain customer-centricity, adapt to changes, and sustain a thriving business.

"**Loyalty** often paves the way for longevity, both in relationships and endeavors"

— Unknown

| L |

LOYALTY = LONGEVITY

# Loyalty = Longevity

The correlation between "being loyalty" and "longevity" suggests that fostering loyalty among customers, employees, partners, and stakeholders can lead to the long-term success and sustainability of a business. Here's how loyalty contributes to obtaining, maintaining, and sustaining a business:

**1. Obtaining Business:**
Building loyal relationships with initial customers and clients can lead to repeat business, referrals, and positive word-of-mouth recommendations, helping you obtain a steady stream of customers.

**2. Customer Retention:**
Loyal customers tend to stay with a business over time, contributing to customer retention. This consistent customer base provides a foundation for ongoing business growth.

**3. Employee Retention:**
Fostering employee loyalty through a positive work environment, recognition, and growth opportunities reduces turnover. Long-term employee relationships lead to improved productivity and institutional knowledge.

**4. Stakeholder Support:**
Gaining loyalty from stakeholders, including investors and partners, can lead to sustained financial support and collaborative efforts that contribute to the long-term health of the business.

Loyalty = Longevity

### **5. Brand Advocacy:**
Loyal customers become brand advocates, spreading positive reviews and recommendations. This organic advocacy attracts new customers and extends the longevity of your business.

### **6. Consistent Revenue:**
Loyal customers contribute to consistent revenue streams, reducing the dependence on sporadic sales spikes and ensuring business stability.

### **7. Trust and Credibility:**
Long-term relationships built on loyalty establish trust and credibility within the industry. This reputation attracts more clients and partners, contributing to business longevity.

### **8. Adaptation and Evolution:**
Loyal employees and stakeholders are more likely to support business adaptation and evolution as the market changes. Their commitment aids in navigating challenges and embracing new opportunities.

### **9. Quality Improvement:**
Feedback from loyal customers and employees can highlight areas for improvement, leading to enhanced products, services, and operational processes over time.

Loyalty = Longevity

**10. Sustainable Growth:**

By focusing on loyalty and customer satisfaction, you establish the foundation for steady growth and long-term success, ensuring the business can weather economic fluctuations.

Loyalty is a key factor in achieving business longevity. Whether it's customer loyalty, employee loyalty, or stakeholder loyalty, building and maintaining these relationships contribute to obtaining, maintaining, and sustaining a successful business over the long haul.

"Effective **management** can be seen as the **matriculation** process, guiding a team or organization towards it goals and success"

— Unknown

# | M |

## MANAGEMENT = MATRICULATION

## Management = Matriculation

The comparison between "being management" and "matriculation" suggests that effectively managing various aspects of a business is essential for its success and growth, similar to progressing through educational levels. Here's how being skilled in management can contribute to obtaining, maintaining, and sustaining a business:

**1. Obtaining Business:**
Implementing effective management strategies, such as well-organized processes and a clear value proposition, can help you obtain initial clients and customers.

**2. Operational Efficiency:**
Efficient management of resources, workflows, and operations ensures that the business runs smoothly and maximizes productivity, contributing to ongoing success.

**3. Strategic Planning:**
Strategic management involves setting clear goals and planning for the future. This strategic approach is essential for obtaining funding, partners, and resources.

**4. Resource Allocation:**
Effective resource allocation, including budgeting and manpower, supports obtaining the necessary tools and personnel to run the business.

Management = Matriculation

### 5. Customer Satisfaction:
Efficiently managing customer interactions, addressing inquiries, and providing quality products/services can lead to satisfied customers who are more likely to continue doing business with you.

### 6. Employee Development:
Proper management includes nurturing a positive work environment, providing growth opportunities, and empowering employees. This leads to a skilled and motivated workforce.

### 7. Adaptation to Change:
Businesses need to adapt to market changes. Effective management allows you to navigate shifts in the industry and adjust strategies for continued success.

### 8. Risk Management:
Skillful management involves identifying and mitigating risks. This approach safeguards the business against potential pitfalls that could hinder success.

### 9. Innovation and Growth:
Active management includes fostering a culture of innovation and seeking new growth opportunities, driving the business forward.

Management = Matriculation

## 10. Long-Term Sustainability:

Like progressing through an educational system, effective management allows the business to "graduate" to higher levels of success and sustainability over time.

Being skilled in business management is comparable to progressing through educational levels—it involves systematic planning, development, and adaptability. Effective management is crucial for obtaining clients, maintaining operational efficiency, sustaining growth, and achieving long-term success in the ever-evolving business landscape.

"**No** means no and respecting that boundary is a fundamental aspect of consent and respect"

— Alex Lanier

| N |

NO = NO

# No = No

The idea that "being no equal no" suggests that the ability to say "no" appropriately and decisively is important for obtaining, maintaining, and sustaining a business. Here's how knowing when and how to say "no" contributes to various aspects of business:

**1. Obtaining Business:**
Knowing when to decline opportunities that don't align with your business goals or values helps you focus on the most relevant and beneficial opportunities, increasing the chances of obtaining the right kind of business.

**2. Resource Allocation:**
Appropriately saying "no" to projects or tasks that are outside your expertise or capacity allows you to allocate resources effectively and maintain the quality of your offerings.

**3. Strategic Focus:**
Saying "no" to distractions or tangential projects helps you maintain a strategic focus on core business objectives, ensuring that you obtain opportunities that contribute to your business's success.

**4. Work-Life Balance:**
Setting boundaries and declining excessive work demands can help you maintain a healthy work-life balance, preventing burnout and sustaining your ability to operate your business effectively.

**5. Customer Alignment:**

## No = No

Politely declining customers or projects that don't align with your business's strengths or values ensures that you maintain a customer base that appreciates your offerings.

### **6. Quality Control:**
Saying "no" to projects that compromise quality or exceed your capacity helps you maintain high standards, safeguarding the quality of your products or services.

### **7. Risk Mitigation:**
Declining partnerships or collaborations that carry substantial risks can prevent potential harm to your business and contribute to its long-term sustainability.

### **8. Focusing on Growth Areas:**
Saying "no" to activities that don't contribute to your business's growth strategy allows you to concentrate resources on areas that have the potential to sustain and expand your business.

### **9. Brand Consistency:**
Politely refusing opportunities that don't align with your brand's image and values helps you maintain brand consistency and reputation.

### **10. Sustainability:**
Making informed decisions about where to invest your time, money, and efforts by saying "no" when necessary supports the long-term sustainability of your business.

The ability to say "no" when appropriate is crucial for obtaining, maintaining, and sustaining business success.

## No = No

By making selective and strategic decisions about where to invest your resources and energy, you can ensure that your business thrives and grows in alignment with your goals and values.

"**Order** creates the **opportunity** for clarity and productivity to flourish"

— Jane Eier

| O |

ORDER = OPPORTUNITY

# Order = Opportunity

The concept that "being order equals opportunity" suggests that maintaining organizational order and structure in your business creates opportunities for obtaining, maintaining, and sustaining success. Here's how a well-ordered approach contributes to various aspects of business:

### 1. Obtaining Business:
A well-organized business presents a professional image, attracting potential clients and partners who see your commitment to excellence and reliability.

### 2. Effective Communication:
Organizational order enhances communication clarity, minimizing misunderstandings and creating opportunities for smoother interactions with clients, employees, and stakeholders.

### 3. Operational Efficiency:
Efficient processes create opportunities for higher productivity and cost savings, allowing you to maximize output and profits.

### 4. Strategic Planning:
Organized strategic planning opens opportunities for identifying new markets, innovative products/services, and growth avenues that align with your business goals.

### 5. Customer Experience:

## Order = Opportunity

A structured approach to customer interactions leads to positive experiences, increasing customer loyalty and repeat business opportunities.

### 6. Employee Empowerment:
Well-defined roles and responsibilities empower employees, creating opportunities for them to excel and contribute effectively to the business.

### 7. Risk Management:
An organized risk management strategy minimizes potential disruptions and maximizes the opportunity to protect your business from unexpected challenges.

### 8. Adaptation to Change:
An orderly business can adapt more readily to changing market conditions, opening opportunities to pivot, innovate, and stay ahead of the competition.

### 9. Long-Term Sustainability:
An organized approach to business operations fosters long-term opportunities for sustainability by ensuring stability and adaptability.

### 10. Expansion and Growth:
Maintaining order positions your business for expansion and growth by creating the foundation for scaling operations, entering new markets, and pursuing new opportunities.

## Order = Opportunity

Embracing order and organizational structure creates opportunities that are vital for obtaining, maintaining, and sustaining business success. By cultivating an environment of efficiency, clear communication, and strategic planning, you can capitalize on various opportunities that contribute to the growth and longevity of your business.

"The best businesses are driven by **purpose**, not profit"

— Roy Spence

# | P |

## PURPOSE = POSITION

# Purpose = Position

The comparison between "being purpose" and "position" suggests that having a clear sense of purpose in your business is closely tied to your positioning in the market, which in turn affects your ability to obtain, maintain, and sustain success. Here's how aligning your purpose with your position contributes to various aspects of business:

### 1. Obtaining Business:
Clarifying your business's purpose helps you position your offerings effectively in the market. When customers understand the value and purpose of your products or services, they are more likely to choose your business.

### 2. Differentiation:
Your business purpose sets you apart from competitors. This unique positioning attracts customers who resonate with your purpose and values.

### 3. Brand Identity:
Your purpose defines your brand identity. A strong brand position built on purpose creates recognition and loyalty among customers.

### 4. Customer Engagement:

Purpose = Position

Businesses with a clear purpose can engage customers on a deeper level by conveying the meaningful impact of their products or services.

**5. Sustainability:**
Aligning your business purpose with your position ensures long-term viability. Sustainable businesses often have a strong sense of purpose that resonates with stakeholders.

**6. Employee Alignment:**
Businesses with a clear purpose attract employees who align with the company's mission. This alignment contributes to a more motivated and engaged workforce.

**7. Innovation:**
A well-defined purpose can guide innovation efforts, allowing your business to develop products or services that meet specific needs and position you as an industry leader.

**8. Customer Loyalty:**
A purpose-driven business builds customer loyalty. When customers connect with your purpose, they are more likely to remain loyal and provide repeat business.

**9. Adaptation:**

Purpose = Position

A purpose-driven position provides a stable foundation for adapting to changing market conditions while staying true to your core values.

**10. Long-Term Impact:**

Purpose-driven businesses often have a larger social impact, which enhances their reputation, attracts customers, and contributes to long-term success.

The alignment of purpose with your business position is crucial for obtaining, maintaining, and sustaining business success. A clear sense of purpose shapes your brand, guides decision-making, attracts customers, and positions you uniquely in the market—factors that collectively contribute to your business's growth and longevity.

"Quality is not an act; it is a habit"

— Aristotle

# | Q |

QUALITY = QUALIFIED

## Quality = Qualified

The comparison between "being quality" and "qualified" suggests that maintaining high-quality products, services, and operations in your business is directly related to being qualified, competent, and successful. Here's how focusing on quality contributes to obtaining, maintaining, and sustaining business success:

**1. Obtaining Business:**
Offering high-quality products or services positions your business as qualified and capable in meeting customer needs, increasing the likelihood of attracting new customers.

**2. Customer Trust:**
Consistently delivering quality builds customer trust in your business's capabilities, leading to repeat business and referrals.

**3. Market Reputation:**
A reputation for quality establishes your business as qualified in its industry, creating a positive perception that can attract new opportunities and partnerships.

**4. Competitive Advantage:**
Maintaining quality gives your business a competitive edge, showcasing your qualifications compared to businesses with lower standards.

**5. Employee Qualifications:**

## Quality = Qualified

Employing qualified staff contributes to maintaining quality standards, which in turn enhances your business's reputation and trustworthiness.

### 6. Consistency:
Consistently delivering high-quality offerings demonstrates that your business is qualified to meet customer expectations and needs over time.

### 7. Customer Satisfaction:
 *Quality Equals Qualified:* High-quality products and services satisfy customers' needs, demonstrating that your business is qualified to provide solutions that deliver value.

### 8. Long-Term Success:
A focus on quality helps sustain business success by ensuring customer loyalty, positive reputation, and enduring relevance in the market.

### 9. Risk Mitigation:
Maintaining quality reduces the risk of errors, recalls, or customer dissatisfaction, demonstrating your qualifications to manage challenges effectively.

### 10. Innovation and Improvement:
A commitment to quality indicates that your business is qualified to innovate, improve, and adapt to changing customer demands.

## Quality = Qualified

Emphasizing quality in your products, services, and operations goes hand-in-hand with being qualified and competent in your industry. This dedication to quality not only helps you obtain and maintain business but also sustains your success over time by building trust, reputation, and customer loyalty.

"**<u>Repetition</u>**, when executed effectively, can lead to increased <u>revenue</u> and brand recognition"

— Olivia Graham

# | R |

REPETITION = REVENUE

Repetition = Revenue

The concept that "repetition equals revenue" suggests that consistently repeating successful strategies, actions, and customer interactions leads to increased revenue and supports obtaining, maintaining, and sustaining business success. Here's how the principle of repetition contributes to various aspects of business:

**1. Obtaining Business:**
Consistently delivering high-quality products or services that meet customer needs encourages repeat business and referrals, contributing to revenue growth.

**2. Customer Loyalty:**
Building strong customer relationships through consistent positive experiences fosters loyalty, increasing the likelihood of repeat purchases and sustained revenue.

**3. Brand Recognition:**
Repetition of branding efforts, marketing messages, and customer engagement activities enhances brand recognition, attracting more customers and generating revenue.

**4. Predictable Income:**
A base of repeat customers provides a steady stream of predictable income, making it easier to forecast and manage finances.

Repetition = Revenue

**5. Cross-Selling and Upselling:**
Repeat interactions with customers create opportunities to cross-sell related products or upsell higher-value offerings, leading to increased revenue per customer.

**6. Efficient Operations:**
Repeating efficient processes and workflows improves productivity, allowing you to serve more customers and generate higher revenue.

**7. Refined Marketing:**
Repetition of marketing campaigns allows you to refine strategies based on what resonates with your audience, leading to more effective revenue-generating efforts.

**8. Customer Advocacy:**
Consistently positive experiences prompt customers to become advocates, sharing their satisfaction with others and bringing in new revenue-generating opportunities.

**9. Long-Term Relationships:**
Consistent repetition builds long-term relationships with customers, suppliers, and partners, resulting in sustained business interactions and revenue streams.

**10. Business Expansion:**

## Repetition = Revenue

Repeating successful expansion strategies in new markets or with new products/services can lead to increased revenue and growth opportunities.
The principle of repetition underscores the importance of consistently delivering value to customers and maintaining positive interactions. By focusing on repetition in various aspects of your business, you create the conditions for repeat business, customer loyalty, brand recognition, and sustained revenue growth, all of which are vital for obtaining, maintaining, and sustaining business success over time.

"**<u>Sustainability</u>** is no longer an option, but a necessity for businesses that want to thrive in the long term"

— John Elkington

| S |

SENSIBILITY = SUSTAINABILITY

# Sensibility = Sustainability

The comparison between "sensibility" and "sustainability" suggests that making sensible and thoughtful decisions in your business practices directly contributes to achieving sustainability and supports obtaining, maintaining, and sustaining business success. Here's how practicing sensibility aligns with sustainability across various aspects of business:

**1. Obtaining Business:**
Making sensible decisions about target markets, products, and pricing strategies helps you obtain business from customers who align with your offerings and values.

**2. Resource Management:**
Sensible resource management, including efficient energy use and waste reduction, contributes to environmental sustainability and cost savings.

**3. Operational Efficiency:**
Implementing sensible processes and workflows improves efficiency, reduces operational waste, and supports long-term business sustainability.

**4. Ethical Practices:**
Making ethically sensible choices in your business practices builds trust with customers, which is crucial for long-term business sustainability.

**5. Customer Relationships:**

## Sensibility = Sustainability

Sensible customer interactions, focused on providing value and addressing needs, lead to lasting relationships and sustained revenue.

### 6. Product Longevity:
Creating products with a focus on quality and durability aligns with sensible consumption practices and contributes to environmental sustainability.

### 7. Innovation:
Thoughtful innovation that addresses real customer needs supports long-term business sustainability by offering relevant solutions.

### 8. Community Engagement:
Sensible community engagement and responsible corporate citizenship build positive relationships and contribute to sustainable business growth.

### 9. Risk Mitigation:
Making sensible decisions in risk management reduces potential liabilities and contributes to the overall stability of the business.

### 10. Long-Term Vision:
Sensible, forward-thinking decision-making considers long-term implications, guiding the business toward sustainable growth and success.

Practicing sensibility in your business operations aligns with the principles of sustainability and contributes to obtaining, maintaining, and sustaining business success. By making thoughtful, ethical, and efficient choices, you

## Sensibility = Sustainability

create a foundation for long-term viability, positive relationships, and responsible growth that benefits your business and the broader community.

"In business, the day you stop becoming **teachable** is the day you start falling behind"

— Richard Branson

# T

## TEACHABLE = TENACIOUS

# Teachable = Tenacious

The comparison between "teachable" and "tenacious" suggests that being open to learning and adaptable while maintaining a determined and persistent attitude is crucial for obtaining, maintaining, and sustaining business success. Here's how being teachable is related to being tenacious across various aspects of business:

### 1. Obtaining Business:
A teachable attitude helps you learn from successes and failures, while being tenacious in pursuing leads and opportunities aids in obtaining new business.

### 2. Adaptation to Market Changes:
A teachable mindset allows you to adapt to changing market conditions, while tenacity ensures you remain committed to your goals despite challenges.

### 3. Customer Feedback:
Being open to customer feedback (teachable) and acting upon it with determination (tenacious) leads to continuous improvement and customer satisfaction.

### 4. Competitor Analysis:
A teachable approach to studying competitors helps you learn from their strategies, while tenacity ensures you keep pursuing innovation and differentiation.

Teachable = Tenacious

### 5. Networking and Relationships:
A teachable demeanor fosters meaningful relationships, while tenacity ensures you nurture and maintain those relationships over time.

### 6. Resilience:
A teachable attitude helps you learn from setbacks, while tenacity empowers you to bounce back and persevere through challenges.

### 7. Skill Development:
Being open to learning new skills (teachable) and persevering through the learning process (tenacious) enhances your expertise and business capabilities.

### 8. Problem Solving:
A teachable mindset encourages seeking knowledge and advice to solve problems, while tenacity drives you to find solutions and overcome obstacles.

### 9. Long-Term Vision:
A teachable and tenacious approach guides you to continuously learn, adapt, and work toward your long-term business vision.

### 10. Innovation:
Being open to learning about emerging trends and technologies (teachable) and persevering through the challenges of innovation (tenacious) lead to business growth.

## Teachable = Tenacious

The combination of being teachable and tenacious creates a powerful approach to business success. Being open to learning and adaptable while maintaining a determined and persistent attitude helps you navigate challenges, make informed decisions, and pursue opportunities, contributing to obtaining, maintaining, and sustaining business success over the long term.

"Your **uniqueness** is your greatest strength. Don't try to fit in; standout"

— Matshona Dhliwayo

| U |

UNIQUENESS = UNLIMITED
OPPORTUNITIES

# Uniqueness = Unlimited Opportunities

The concept that "uniqueness equals unlimited opportunities" suggests that having a unique and distinct value proposition opens the door to a wide range of opportunities for obtaining, maintaining, and sustaining business success. Here's how uniqueness contributes to various aspects of business:

### 1. Maintaining Business:
A unique offering sets you apart from competitors, making it easier to attract customers who are intrigued by your distinctive products or services.

### 2. Market Differentiation:
Uniqueness helps you stand out in the market, creating opportunities for your business to be noticed and chosen over alternatives.

### 3. Customer Attraction:
A unique value proposition attracts customers seeking something different, increasing your chances of obtaining new business.

### 4. Innovation and Creativity:
Being unique encourages continuous innovation and creative problem-solving, leading to opportunities for growth and improvement.

### 5. Partnerships and Collaborations:

## Uniqueness = Unlimited Opportunities

Other businesses may seek to collaborate with you due to your unique offerings, leading to new partnerships and revenue streams.

### 6. Niche Markets:
Uniqueness allows you to target specific niche markets, where competition is lower and opportunities to meet unique needs are higher.

### 7. Brand Attractiveness:
A unique brand identity attracts customers who resonate with your values and aesthetics, leading to long-term business opportunities.

### 8. Customer Loyalty:
Unique offerings foster customer loyalty, as customers are more likely to return to a business that provides distinct value.

### 9. Adaptability:
Being unique enhances your adaptability, allowing you to pivot and explore different avenues as market trends change.

### 10. Long-Term Sustainability:
A unique business model, product, or approach can sustain interest and relevance over time, contributing to long-term business success.

## Uniqueness = Unlimited Opportunities

Uniqueness sets the stage for an array of opportunities in business. By offering something

distinct, you create a valuable position in the market that attracts customers, partners, and collaborators. This uniqueness not only helps you obtain business initially but also maintains customer interest and sustains your business's success over the long term.

"In business, credibility and **validity** are earned through consistency and integrity"

— Thomas Dunhill

# | V |

VERIFIED = VALIDITY

# Verified = Validity

The correlation between "verified" and "validity" suggests that ensuring authenticity, accuracy, and credibility in your business practices leads to valid and trustworthy operations. Here's how the concept of being verified relates to validity across various aspects of business:

### 1. Obtaining Business:
Being verified, such as through certifications or positive reviews, validates your business's credibility and can attract new customers seeking trustworthy options.

### 2. Credible Information:
Providing accurate and verified information about your products, services, and business history enhances the validity of your claims, fostering customer trust.

### 3. Compliance and Regulations:
Adhering to verified compliance standards ensures the validity of your business practices and protects your reputation.

### 4. Customer Reviews and Testimonials:
Verified customer reviews and testimonials add validity to your offerings, as they provide real-world evidence of your business's value.

### 5. Data Accuracy:

## Verified = Validity

Using verified data and information in your marketing and decision-making enhances the validity of your strategies and initiatives.

### **6. Brand Reputation:**
Verified positive brand reputation and customer feedback validate your business's quality, encouraging customer loyalty and repeat business.

### **7. Ethical Practices:**
Upholding verified ethical practices adds validity to your commitment to social responsibility and fosters a positive brand image.

### **8. Contractual Agreements:**
Verified and legally sound contractual agreements validate business transactions, protecting both parties and maintaining trust.

### **9. Product Authenticity:**
Verified product authenticity ensures the validity of the value customers receive, fostering customer satisfaction and loyalty.

### **10. Long-Term Trust:**
Building and maintaining verified credibility and authenticity leads to long-term trust, which sustains customer relationships and business success.

The concept of being verified is closely linked to the validity and trustworthiness of your business. By

## Verified = Validity

consistently ensuring authenticity, accuracy, and credibility in your practices, you create a valid and reliable image that contributes to obtaining, maintaining, and sustaining business success over time.

"**Waste** is worse than loss."

— Thomas Edison

| W |

WASTE NOT = WANT NOT

## Waste Not = Want Not

The phrase "waste not, want not" emphasizes the importance of avoiding wastefulness in order to prevent shortages and ensure long-term abundance. In the context of business, this principle can be applied to obtaining, maintaining, and sustaining success through efficient resource management. Here's how "waste not" relates to "want not" in the business context:

**1. Resource Management:**
Efficiently managing resources, such as materials, time, and finances, prevents wastage and ensures that you have what you need to operate effectively.

**2. Cost Control:**
Minimizing wasteful spending and unnecessary expenses helps you maintain financial stability and avoid shortages of funds in the future.

**3. Operational Efficiency:**
Streamlining processes and workflows reduces inefficiencies, ensuring that your business operates smoothly and avoids unnecessary delays.

**4. Sustainable Practices:**
Adopting environmentally conscious practices reduces waste and promotes sustainability, ensuring that natural resources are available for future generations.

**5. Customer Satisfaction:**

## Waste Not = Want Not

Efficiently meeting customer needs and minimizing errors prevents dissatisfaction and ensures that customers continue to support your business.

**6. Inventory Management:**
Properly managing inventory levels prevents overstocking or shortages, ensuring that you have the right products available when customers want them.

**7. Energy Conservation:**
Practicing energy efficiency reduces waste and lowers utility costs, ensuring that you have resources for other business needs.

**8. Time Utilization:**
Efficient time management prevents wastage of valuable hours and ensures that you can dedicate time to strategic initiatives and growth.

**9. Innovation and Improvement:**
Identifying areas of waste encourages continuous improvement, leading to innovations that create new opportunities and prevent stagnation.

**10. Long-Term Sustainability:**
Adopting waste reduction strategies contributes to the long-term sustainability of your business, preventing resource shortages and promoting growth.

## Waste Not = Want Not

The principle of "waste not, want not" encourages efficient resource management, which is crucial for obtaining, maintaining, and sustaining business success. By minimizing wastage and making the most of your resources, you create a foundation for stable operations, cost savings, customer satisfaction, and long-term growth.

"Don't make **eXcuses**, make improvements."

— Thomas Edison

# |X|

eXCUSES = NO eXECUTION

## eXcuses = no eXecution

The equation "excuses equal no execution" suggests that when excuses are made instead of taking action, it results in a lack of progress and accomplishment. In the context of business, excuses can hinder the ability to obtain, maintain, and sustain success. Here's how the principle of no execution due to excuses relates to various aspects of business:

### 1. Obtaining Business:
Making excuses instead of pursuing opportunities or leads can prevent you from obtaining new business or clients.

### 2. Proactive Problem-Solving:
Avoiding action through excuses hampers your ability to proactively address challenges and find solutions, which is essential for business success.

### 3. Customer Relationships:
Making excuses instead of resolving customer issues may damage relationships and hinder your ability to maintain customer satisfaction.

### 4. Innovation:
Focusing on excuses rather than innovative thinking prevents the execution of new ideas that can drive business growth.

### 5. Risk Taking:

eXcuses = no eXecution

Averse to taking calculated risks due to excuses can hinder your ability to explore new opportunities and expand the business.

**6. Project Completion:**
Allowing excuses to delay or halt projects leads to incomplete initiatives and missed opportunities for progress.

**7. Adaptation to Change:**
Embracing excuses over change prevents the execution of strategies needed to adapt to evolving market conditions.

**8. Employee Engagement:**
Making excuses instead of addressing employee concerns affects morale and inhibits the execution of a motivated workforce.

**9. Long-Term Planning:**
Relying on excuses rather than executing strategic plans limits your ability to sustain business growth over time.

**10. Personal Development:**
Making excuses instead of pursuing ongoing personal and professional development hinders your ability to lead and make informed decisions.

## eXcuses = no eXecution

The tendency to make excuses instead of taking action can hinder progress and success in various aspects of business. By adopting a mindset of execution and proactively addressing challenges, you create opportunities to obtain, maintain, and sustain business success over the long term.

"In business, **yielding** can be a strategic move. Sometimes it is better to bend than to break."

— Unknown

| Y |

YEARNING = YIELDING

## Yearning = Yielding

The equation "yearning equals yielding" implies that having a strong desire or yearning to achieve something is directly connected to the ability to produce results or yield outcomes. In the context of business, this principle emphasizes the importance of determination and focused effort. Here's how yearning is related to yielding across various aspects of business:

### 1. Obtaining Business:
A strong yearning to succeed drives proactive efforts to obtain new business opportunities, resulting in successful outcomes.

### 2. Customer Satisfaction:
A genuine yearning to satisfy customer needs and exceed expectations often leads to positive customer experiences and long-term loyalty.

### 3. Innovation:
A yearning for innovation motivates you to explore new ideas and solutions, yielding novel products, services, or processes that can drive business growth.

### 4. Problem Solving:
A deep yearning to address challenges leads to persistent problem-solving efforts, ultimately yielding effective solutions.

### 5. Relationship Building:

## Yearning = Yielding

A yearning to build meaningful relationships with clients, partners, and stakeholders often yields collaborations, partnerships, and business growth opportunities.

### 6. Employee Engagement:
A genuine yearning to engage and motivate employees yields higher productivity, job satisfaction, and a positive work environment.

### 7. Adaptation to Change:
A strong yearning to adapt to changing market conditions drives efforts to adjust strategies and tactics, yielding continued relevance and success.

### 8. Strategic Planning:
A yearning for long-term success drives meticulous strategic planning, leading to well-executed initiatives and desired outcomes.

### 9. Personal Growth:
A yearning for personal growth and development yields increased leadership capabilities, decision-making skills, and business acumen.

### 10. Market Expansion:
A yearning to enter new markets or expand geographically can yield successful market penetration and business growth.

## Yearning = Yielding

The equation "yearning equals yielding" emphasizes that a strong desire to achieve specific outcomes drives the focused efforts needed to obtain, maintain, and sustain business success. By channeling your yearning into strategic actions and persistent determination, you create opportunities to yield positive results, growth, and long-term success in the business landscape.

"**Zero investment** often means zero commitment, and that rarely leads to significant outcomes."

— Unknown

# | Z |

ZERO INVESTMENT = ZERO RETURN

# Zero Investment = Zero Return

The statement "zero investment equals zero return" underscores the principle that in business, expecting returns without making investments—whether they're financial, time-related, or effort-based—is unrealistic. Here's how this principle applies to obtaining, maintaining, and sustaining business success:

**1. Obtaining Business:**
Without investing in marketing, networking, or product development, you'll likely struggle to attract new customers and obtain business.

**2. Quality and Innovation:**
Failing to invest in improving product quality and innovation can result in a lack of differentiation and reduced customer interest.

**3. Customer Engagement:**
Neglecting efforts to engage and build relationships with customers can lead to reduced loyalty and fewer repeat purchases.

**4. Employee Development:**
Not investing in employee training and growth can result in lower morale, decreased productivity, and a lack of skilled talent.

**5. Marketing and Branding:**

## Zero Investment = Zero Return

Without investing in marketing and branding efforts, you're less likely to create brand awareness and attract new customers.

### 6. Market Research:
Failing to invest in market research can lead to uninformed decisions, missed opportunities, and potential losses.

### 7. Technology and Infrastructure:
Neglecting investments in technology and infrastructure can hinder operational efficiency and limit scalability.

### 8. Risk Management:
Not investing in risk management strategies can lead to unforeseen challenges that hinder business growth and success.

### 9. Innovation and Adaptation:
Without investing in innovation and adapting to market changes, your business may become stagnant and less competitive.

### 10. Long-Term Sustainability:
Failing to invest in long-term strategies and business development efforts can lead to a lack of sustainability and future growth.

The principle "zero investment equals zero return" highlights that expecting significant business

## Zero Investment = Zero Return

outcomes without making appropriate investments is unrealistic. To obtain, maintain, and sustain business success, it's important to strategically invest resources, time, and effort into various aspects of your business. These investments create opportunities for growth, differentiation, customer loyalty, and long-term viability, contributing to a positive business trajectory.

Which LETTER resonated with where you are in business?

# | Conclusion |

In conclusion, "The ABC's of Business: How to Obtain, Sustain, and Maintain Business from A-Z" serves as a comprehensive guide to navigating the multifaceted world of entrepreneurship. From the initial steps of obtaining business opportunities to the ongoing efforts of sustaining and maintaining growth, this book has explored a diverse range of strategies and concepts.

Throughout its pages, readers have discovered that success in business isn't just about mastering one aspect; it's about understanding the intricate interplay between different elements. Just as the alphabet forms the foundation of language, the A-Z principles outlined in this book form the foundation of a successful business journey.

As readers, you've explored the significance of adaptation, innovation, and perseverance. You've learned that obtaining business opportunities requires a keen eye for potential, while sustaining growth demands a commitment to customer satisfaction and quality. Maintaining business success involves not only managing resources but also nurturing a positive company culture.

## Conclusion

As you close this book, remember that your journey as an entrepreneur is ongoing. The road ahead will have its challenges, but armed with the insights from these pages, you're better equipped to navigate them. Embrace change, remain open to learning, and continuously seek ways to improve your business.

Thank you for embarking on this journey through "The ABC's of Business." May the lessons you've gained serve as a compass as you venture into the dynamic and rewarding world of business, always striving to obtain, sustain, and maintain success from A to Z.

## | About The Author |

**Teia Acker [Moore] is a resilient business-woman, author and media personality who relentlessly balances various aspects of entrepreneurship, motherhood and godly living. She serves a motivational speaker on various platforms to include her podcast #GETNOTICED!**

A native of Savannah, Georgia, Teia Acker [Moore] has always had a passion for helping others. In 2004, Teia graduated from Georgia Southern University with a dual Bachelor's degree in Health Science (Community Health) and Kinesiology (Exercise Science). While there, she received the "President's List Award for achieving a perfect 4.0 GPA in one Semester. Although becoming a physical therapist was a lifelong dream for Teia, she decided to pursue a career in community health after engaging in an internship in the public health sector of a local hospital. It was there where she discovered the essence of helping others and engaging a network of community services into meeting and servicing the needs of its people.

Determined to make a significant difference, Teia set out to pursue a Master's Degree in Business Administration from The University of Phoenix. She graduated in the top 10% of her class in December

## About The Author

of 2008. Faced with the dilemma of inexperience in the business sector, Teia decided to create a business of her own; one that would not only establish her in the business arena, but one that would also enable her to make a difference within her community. She is the owner of the Savannah – based business Ebony & Ivory Professional Services, Incorporated. She is currently enrolled as a doctoral candidate in Business Administration at Walden University.

In addition, Teia is the host of the populated podcast "GETNOTICED" which is currently on 20 stations to include Tidal, Spotify, I Heart Radio, and iTunes. The podcast aids in helping small business owner, entrepreneur and leaders understand the facets of business and the tools needed to sustain and obtain longevity. Teia is also the CEO and Editor of RESILIENT MAGAZINE - a magazine designed to Impact, Empower and Outline the resiliency of African American Women. In her spare time, Teia helps to empower women through her Teia Acker #RESILIENT platform under the title "I AM RESILIENT".

Aside from working in the professional realm, Teia also gives time to the spiritual realm as well. Teia is an active member of First Tabernacle Missionary Baptist Church under the pastoral governance of Pastor Andre Osborne.

Teia is married to James L. Moore, Sr. and is the mother of her amazing son, Trey (15), and her beautiful daughter, Trinity (13). She is an outstanding bonus mom to 4 incredible children: Jaylen (21), James, Jr. (16), Jamaii (15), and Madison (12).

## Connect With ME!

Connect with EIPS‼
📞 404.965.8210
✉ info@ebonyivoryps.com
🚩 P.O. Box 1784 Rincon, Georgia 31326
🌐 www.ebonyivoryps.com

Connect with Teia Acker #RESILIENT‼
📞 713.969.5459
✉ info@teiaacker.com
🚩 P.O. Box 1784 Rincon, Georgia 31326
🌐 www.teiaacker.com

Connect with Resilient Magazine‼
📞 713.969.5459
✉ info@resilientmagazine.com
🚩 P.O. Box 1784 Rincon, Georgia 31326
🌐 www.resilientmagazine.com

Made in the USA
Columbia, SC
21 October 2023

a8db22ef-81b7-4cb5-955d-d43e1a040a33R01